T0084076

INTRODUCTION

Welcome to *Fingerstyle Fitness*, your manual to help master the techniques and styles of players like Merle Travis, Chet Atkins, Leo Kottke, and Tommy Emmanuel. These great players took fingerstyle guitar playing to the next level. Since there's enough fingerstyle repertoire available, this book instead will focus on exercises that will help develop your technique to better play those pieces. Having played the instrument for 40 years, and having developed proficiency in everything from classical to heavy metal, I will present to you the methods I used to hone my chops to get my fingerstyle playing in shape.

HOW TO USE THIS BOOK

Since this book will focus primarily on exercises, I encourage you to refine your practice skills. Many times, when working on a piece of music, the tendency will be to attempt to play the piece up to tempo too early. Having that recording played at a blistering tempo can sometimes be the dangling carrot that we are too eager to grab. I find with pure exercises, there is less of a tendency to play them too fast as there isn't that gold-standard recording that we're all striving to imitate. That being said, it is of utmost importance to always play these exercises with perfect, tension-free execution. Any time we repeat something, we are training our bodies to exactly match our execution. In other words, by repeating an exercise sloppily, you are simply training your fingers to play sloppily. Practice does not make perfect; practice makes permanent! Put your ego aside and put in the time now to play these exercises under control. When you speed them up, your technique and execution will be effortless. I know from experience the damage that playing a piece too fast can do. In my early days of learning classical guitar, I was so determined to be able to play some challenging pieces up to speed that I just kept forcing the technique. To this day, I still have trouble with those pieces. I ingrained bad technique, and it's really hard to fix. I have since learned much more difficult pieces the correct way and can now play them effortlessly; and, if memory serves me right, it took less time and effort to master them with proper practice techniques. I harp on this with all my students, so please forgive me if I keep mentioning it throughout the book! I have found that the most important lesson I can teach students is not "what" but "how."

Each exercise in the book will have an accompanying demonstration video that can be viewed online. For longer pieces, the videos include a slow version followed by a faster version. To view these videos, go to www.halleonard.com/mylibrary and enter the code found on page 1 of this book (title page). You can either stream the videos or download them all to your computer.

RIGHT-HAND CONCEPTS OVERVIEW

If you've watched any other fingerstyle players, you've probably noticed their right-hand technique. You may have also noticed that no two players look exactly the same in regard to the right hand. I would like to address some of these differences.

FINGERSTYLE FITNESS

Effective Workouts for the Fingerstyle Guitarist

To access video, visit:
www.halleonard.com/mylibrary

Enter Code
7603-7934-5890-6825

ISBN 978-1-54007-181-1

Copyright © 2023 by HAL LEONARD LLC
International Copyright Secured All Rights Reserved

No part of this publication may be reproduced in any form or by
any means without the prior written permission of the Publisher.

Visit Hal Leonard Online at
www.halleonard.com

World headquarters, contact:
Hal Leonard
7777 West Bluemound Road
Milwaukee, WI 53213
Email: info@halleonard.com

In Europe, contact:
Hal Leonard Europe Limited
1 Red Place
London, W1K 6PL
Email: info@halleonardeurope.com

In Australia, contact:
Hal Leonard Australia Pty. Ltd.
4 Lentara Court
Cheltenham, Victoria, 3192 Australia
Email: info@halleonard.com.au

A general rule of thumb is to have the right hand positioned in a way that allows the fingers to be perpendicular to the strings. This will allow you to pluck the strings in the most efficient way. Keep the wrist aligned with the forearm, avoid bending it excessively, and keep some space between the wrist and the top of the guitar. The only time this position will really change much is when we're palm muting notes, as that requires the wrist to be closer to the guitar. Although there are some players who are exceptions to the rule, you'll notice most adopt this right-hand position.

But that may be where the similarities end. First off, you may see some players anchoring their hand by lightly touching the pinky to the top of the guitar, while some players prefer that the hand just floats. There is no right or wrong way. In fact, depending on the demands of the piece, I use both techniques. As long as you're not introducing any tension, it won't be a problem to anchor your hand by placing the pinky on the top of the guitar—and perhaps "anchor" isn't the best term to use, although that's the common way to refer to it. If you notice some of the great players using an anchor, the pinky is not planted hard, but rather it just lightly comes in contact with the guitar and moves around as the hand changes position. So, what are the benefits to anchoring? I find it helps with precision and stability, as it gives a bit of a reference point on the guitar.

You may also notice that some players grow out their right-hand nails a bit (perhaps even applying an acrylic coating) and pluck the string with a combination of nails and flesh, while others keep their nails shorts and just use the flesh of the finger to pluck. In the classical world, it is widely accepted that nails are to be used. But again, there are players who don't use nails. In the steel-string fingerstyle world, it is more split. Some do, some don't. I used to use nails, but in the last few years have switched to flesh. Even when I play classical guitar, I am using just flesh. I never had great nails anyway, as they were thin and grew out hooked—and playing on steel strings wore them down very quickly. So, it's really a personal preference. If you prefer the feel and clear tone that nails produce, go for it. If not, flesh will be fine. Always keep the fretting-hand nails short though because they can catch on the strings or even the fretboard.

When playing fingerstyle, we use two different techniques with the right hand: *free stroke* and *rest stroke*. Free stroke is when we pluck the note with a finger, and the finger follows through without touching the adjacent string. When using a rest stroke, we direct the movement of the finger downward into the guitar, and after plucking, the finger comes to "rest" on the adjacent string. The rest stroke is used more frequently in classical guitar, but it does have its place in steel-string fingerstyle guitar. In general, I would say that free stroke is used 90% of the time. Rest stroke is most often used when playing a single-note melody. Because of the downward direction of the stroke, it tends to produce a fuller sound than a free stroke. It's not well suited for *arpeggios* or playing two notes together as the "resting" will mute the ringing strings. To execute a rest stroke, simply adjust your right-hand position to be a bit less perpendicular to the guitar. This will allow you to use the same motions, but the change in position will direct the finger to come to rest on the next string as opposed to clearing it.

That brings us to the final variation among players: to use a thumbpick or not. Coming from a classical background, I resisted the thumbpick for a long time. As I got more into the Chet Atkins style, I decided to give it a go. It really felt awkward for the first few weeks, but soon after, it felt completely natural... That brings up another point that I want to stress: when trying out a new technique, make sure you give it time before you dismiss it. Sometimes I'll suggest something to a student that I feel will be a more efficient way to play. At first it feels awkward, and the student says, "I think it's easier the old way." I encourage them to give it some time as it is a new technique and will feel awkward at first but in the end will be better. Change is never easy, especially when we're used to doing something a certain way... Getting back to the thumbpick, again it is personal preference. Some things will definitely be easier though; if you're trying to get that snappy thump on a palm muted bass note, the thumbpick will really help bring it out. For me, it's a song-by-song decision. I have no problem switching back and forth from using a thumbpick or going without. So, the moral of the story with all these variations is: feel free to try them out and incorporate them into your style. They don't have to define the player.

The fingers of the right hand will be identified in the music with the following letters:

p = thumb

i = index finger

m = middle finger

a = ring finger

These letters or abbreviations come from the Spanish names for the fingers and are used in classical guitar notation; *p* = *pulgar*, *i* = *indice*, *m* = *medio*, and *a* = *anular*. It's helpful to label the right-hand fingers differently than the left-hand fingers, using letters instead of numerals so that there is no confusion. Typically, the right-hand pinky is not used for fingerpicking aside from its use in some flamenco techniques. In that case, notes to be played by the pinky are labeled as *c* (*chico*).

This book is written from the perspective of a right-handed guitarist (where the right hand plucks and the left hand frets). If you are a left-handed player, simply reverse the directions.

EXTRA DEMANDS FOR THE LEFT HAND

Although this book will primarily focus on the techniques of the right hand, fingerstyle guitar playing also introduces some challenges for the left (or fretting) hand. Instead of just playing single-note melodies, many times we'll be playing melodies while holding down bass notes. This can be very challenging at first if you're not used to the feeling of holding down a finger while other fingers are fretting notes. Also, many times the chords we're using in a fingerstyle piece will be more complex than your standard strummed chords. Not to mention, we'll be transitioning through some of these chords more often than in a standard strummed song. Fear not, we've got you covered! There's an entire chapter focused on some development exercises for the left hand, and these exercises will help in every area of your playing, not just fingerstyle. I feel like the strength and dexterity I've gotten from working on fingerstyle pieces has helped make my left hand more capable in all my guitar playing.

DEMONSTRATION VIDEOS

Each example includes a corresponding demonstration video.
To access the videos, just head over to **www.halleonard.com/mylibrary**
and input the unique code found on page 1 of this book!

RIGHT HAND

ARPEGGIOS

Arpeggios are simply the notes of a chord played in succession, either ascending or descending. These will be the simplest exercises in the book but are a cornerstone of solid fingerstyle technique. Many of these exercises will be variations of the *120 Right Hand Studies* by Mauro Giuliani. These studies are required repertoire for the classical guitarist, but the techniques cross over well for the steel-string player. So that the focus remains on the right hand, we'll use a simple and consistent chord progression. Practice holding down not only the notes that are needed but also the entire chord. I've found that holding down the full chord can be a nice "insurance policy" against accidentally brushing an incorrect adjacent note—a great safety measure to help keep things sounding musical. While these next examples don't cover every possible arpeggio, they will be a good introduction to some of the more common ones and will help develop the dexterity needed to play any arpeggio shape.

Exercise 1

Exercise 2

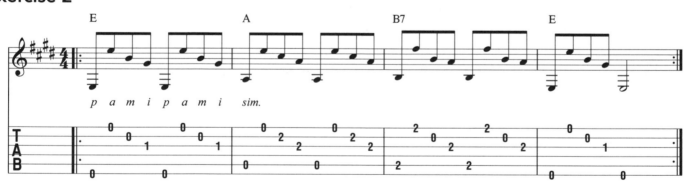

Exercise 3

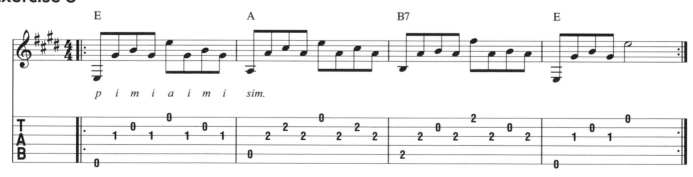

Exercise 4

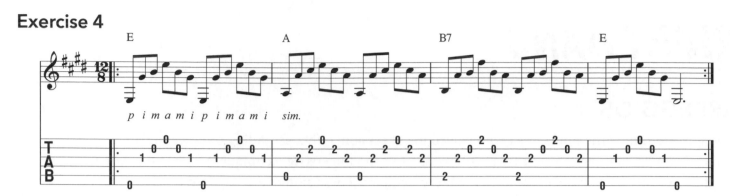

As an added bonus to help challenge the left hand and give the ear a break from the same chord progression, try the previous exercises with different chords, still using the same patterns. The pattern used on the top three notes will always be the same for the right hand, but you'll need to make adjustments with the thumb for the different positions of the bass notes in each chord. Here's an example to get you started.

Exercise 5

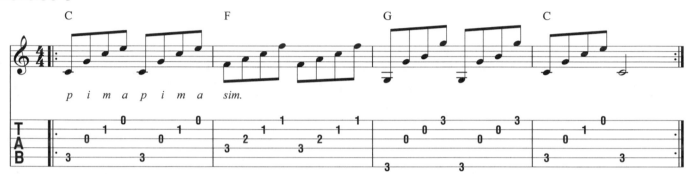

PLAYING TWO NOTES TOGETHER

When playing two notes together with the fingers (*i-m*, *m-a*, or *i-a*), the goal is to pluck the two strings at the same time. Although arpeggiating the notes is a valid interpretive technique, aim for plucking the notes together in these exercises. Use arpeggiation when you want to add more musical flavor to a piece. At first, it may be helpful to use a different sort of planting technique than discussed earlier, one where you place the right-hand fingers on the strings that you intend to pluck in preparation. This planting technique will also create a rest in between the notes.

Exercise 6

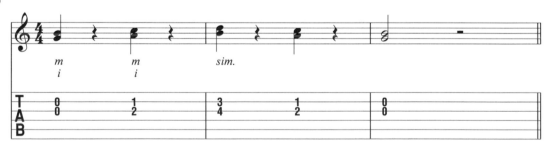

Exercise 7

Make sure you're not only playing both notes at the same time, but also that you can clearly hear both notes. Being able to bring out one note louder than the other is a worthy and difficult technique, but we'll want to use it with purpose. For now, concentrate on even volume for both notes. You can continue to use the planting technique on the following exercises, but it will create a choppier sound; the goal is to be able to make these notes sound more connected. Once you feel comfortable with planting and plucking the notes, work towards being able to pluck them without planting.

Here's a C major scale harmonized in thirds. It makes a great double-note study exercise. The right-hand fingering is shown as *i-m* but try using *m-a* as well.

Exercise 8

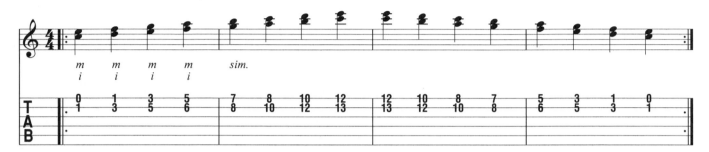

Major-scale study is never time wasted, so here's a G major scale in thirds. Again, use both *i-m* (as shown) and *m-a*.

Exercise 9

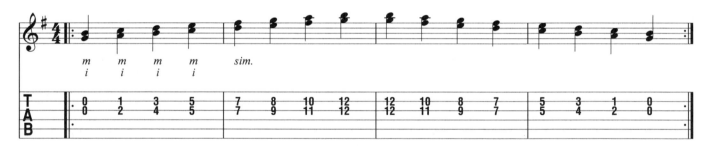

We can also use non-adjacent fingers, *i* and *a*, to pluck double notes.

Exercise 10

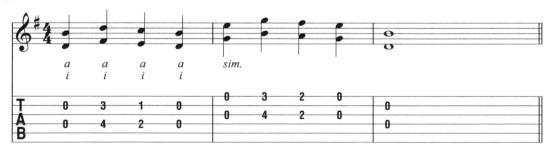

The following exercises use a combination of fingerings for playing double notes.

Exercise 11

Exercise 12

We can also play double notes by using the thumb and a finger. Here's an exercise using a few finger-thumb combinations with a C major chord.

Exercise 13

Although the thumb usually handles the lowest three strings, did you notice how we can also use it on higher strings? There's no "rule of thumb" (pun intended) on when to use it or not. It really depends on the technical demands of the music and the effect you are trying to achieve. Let's go back and revisit some previous exercises, this time incorporating the thumb. Let's repeat each example three times. On the first time, use *p-i*, second time use *p-m*, and on the third time, alternate between *p-i* and *p-m*.

Exercise 14

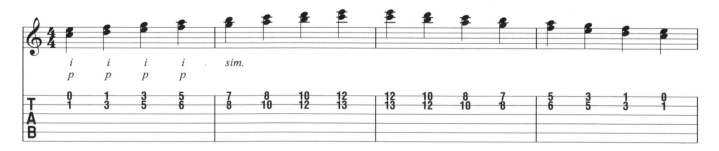

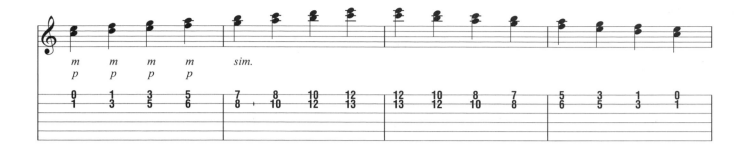

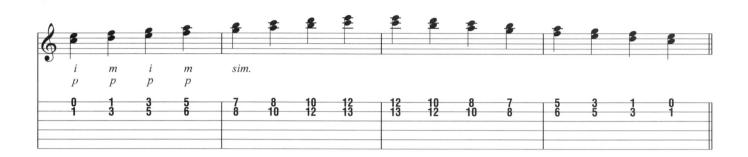

Exercise 15

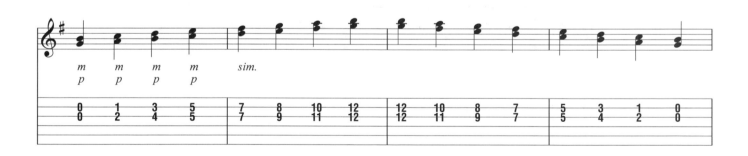

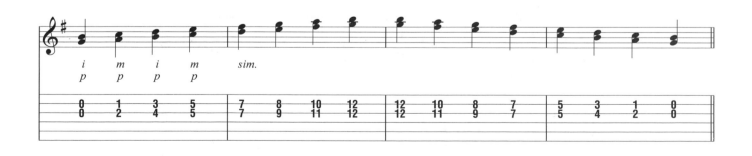

Exercise 16

Now, let's try a few exercises that add double notes to an arpeggio pattern.

Exercise 17

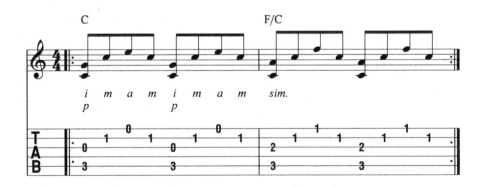

Exercise 18

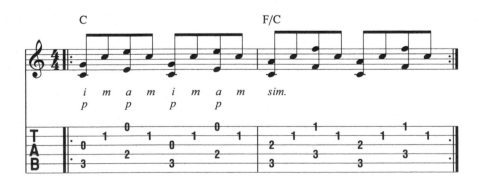

Exercise 19

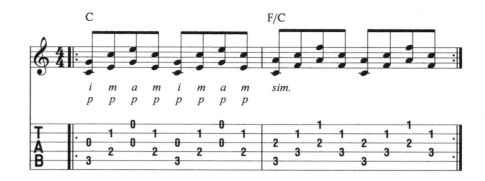

Exercise 20

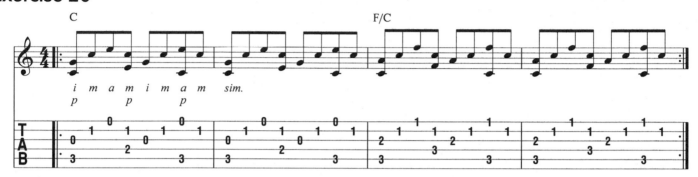

Following are some exercises in playing block chords with the thumb and fingers. We'll start off simple and progress with some muting, syncopation, and bass runs.

Exercise 21

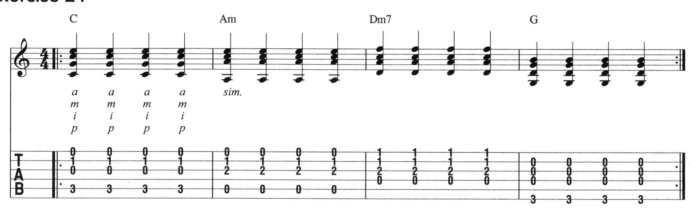

Note the rests on the next example. Use the planting technique with the thumb and fingers to stop the strings from ringing. In some cases, you'll have to plant on the strings you just played and then move the thumb and fingers to a new string group for the next chord.

Exercise 22

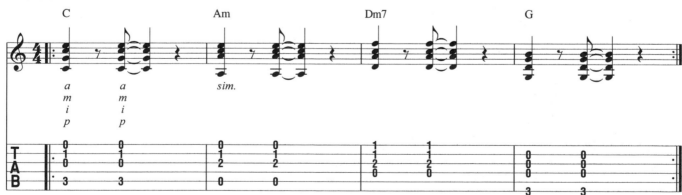

Now, we'll separate the fingers and thumb a bit and add some bass runs.

Exercise 23

Finally, let's put together all the techniques we've discussed into a longer musical piece. Throughout the piece, use *p* on the bottom three strings, *i* on the G string, *m* on the B string, and *a* on the high E string.

Exercise 24

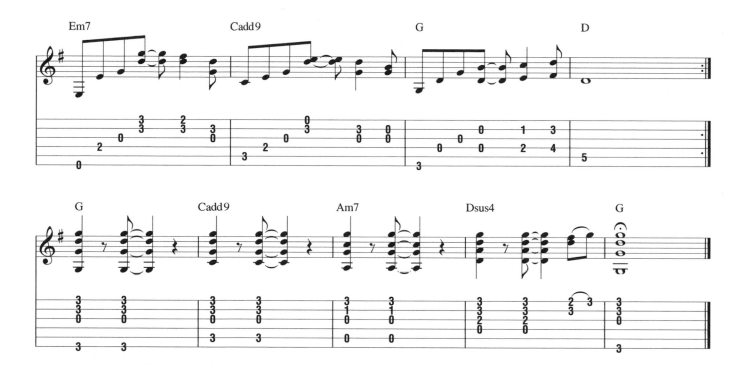

TRAVIS PICKING

Travis picking is named after the famous guitarist Merle Travis. It involves playing steady, alternating bass notes with the thumb while the fingers pluck the higher strings. Although named after Merle Travis, many other players including Chet Atkins, Leo Kottke, James Taylor, and Tommy Emmanuel—just to name a few—have popularized this style. We'll start off here with just the thumb, alternating between bass notes. This is the simplest version of what the thumb does in Travis picking, using only two strings per chord. Later, we'll add a more complicated variation with the thumb alternating between three strings. Even though we're only playing a few notes, hold down the full chord. If you haven't tried a thumbpick yet, this would be a great time since it really lends itself well to Travis picking, helping to articulate those bass notes. In the videos, now, I'll be demonstrating with a thumbpick. But, if you prefer not to use a thumbpick, no problem!

Exercise 25

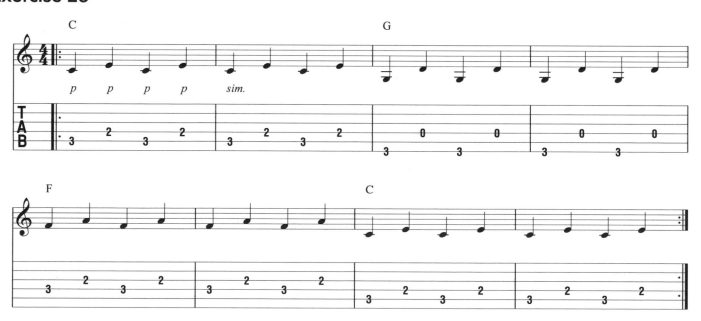

Repeat that last exercise until it feels very natural and you don't have to think about it. Once you've got it down, we can add some melody notes played with the fingers and a bit of syncopation. *Syncopation* refers to the displacement of expected accents within a metrical pattern. Keep that thumb pounding out those solid quarter notes!

Exercise 26

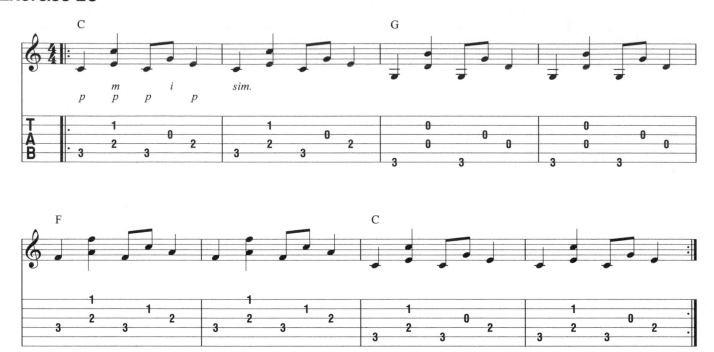

You may have noticed that during the slow version on the last video, the *a* finger rested on the high E string. Resting on a string like this is a totally acceptable thing to do to help keep the strings from ringing and maintain hand position—just make sure it's not introducing any tension to the hand. Now, let's take that same pattern and use it in a different key.

Exercise 27

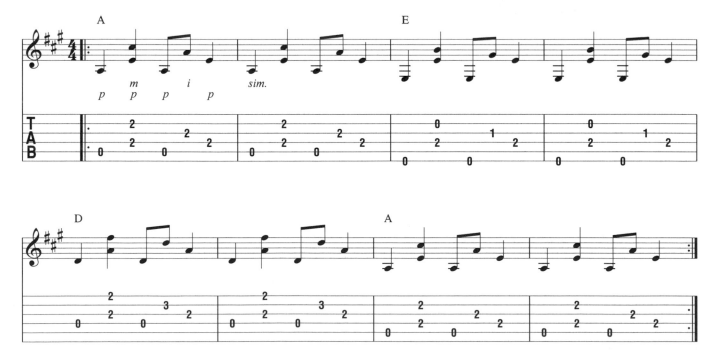

Let's add a few more notes on the top end for these next examples. Remember to keep those bass notes played with the thumb nice and steady.

Exercise 28

Exercise 29

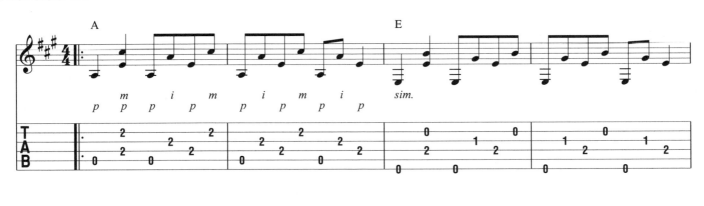

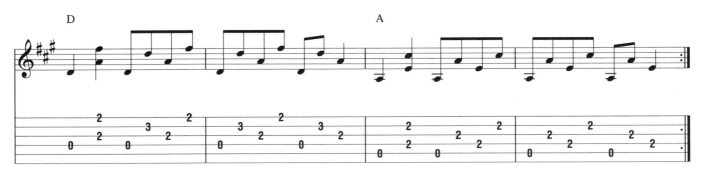

We can also add some complexity to what the thumb plays. Instead of playing just two strings, we can add a third string, which really defines the Travis-picking sound. Here's an exercise using just the thumb in this way. Again, make sure this feels super comfortable and automatic before moving on and adding the fingers in the exercises that follow.

Exercise 30

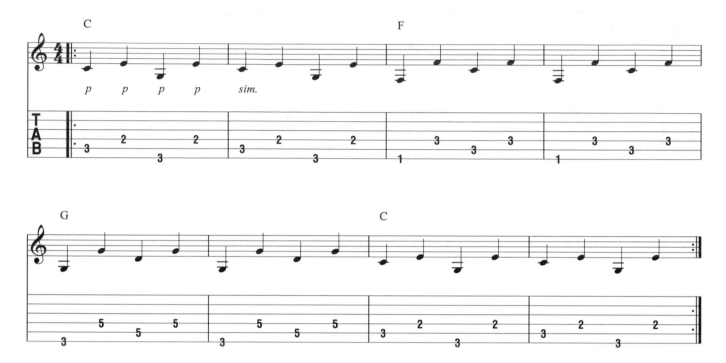

Keep that thumb pattern going, now adding some notes for the fingers to play.

Exercise 31

Exercise 32

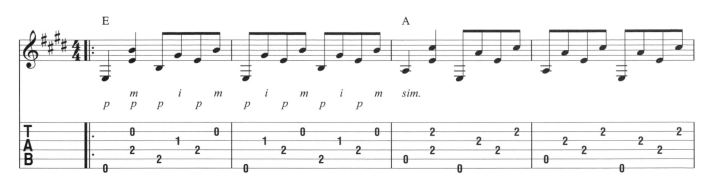

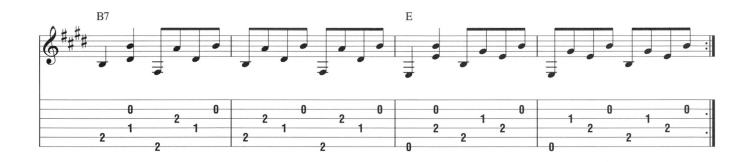

Exercise 33

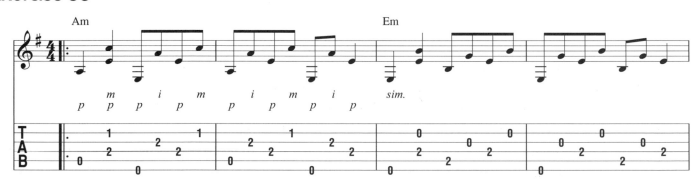

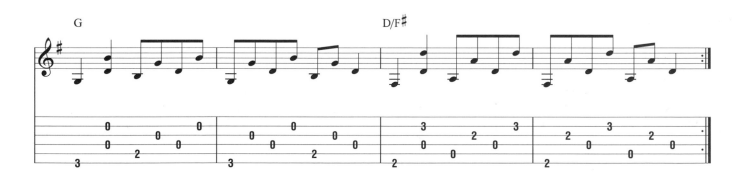

We can also add a palm mute on the thumb notes to help bring out that classic "boom-chick-boom-chick" sound. Make sure the pad of the right hand is only muting the notes played by the thumb. The upper notes should remain unmuted and be left to ring clearly.

Exercise 34

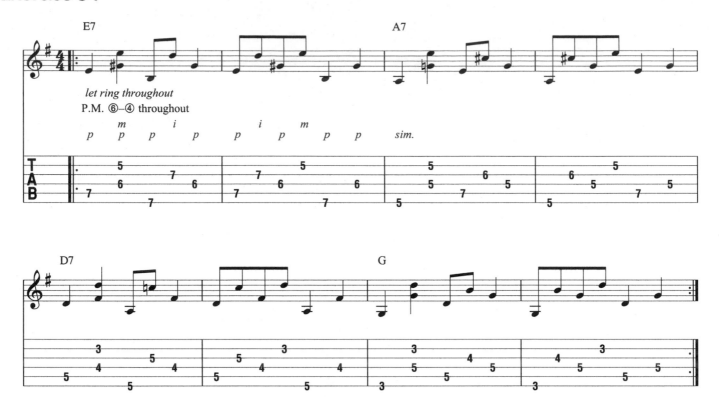

So far, all our melody notes when Travis picking have been found within the basic chord shape. These next exercises will add melody notes that aren't part of the basic chord shape. As always, try to hold down as many notes as possible so that everything rings together nicely. If you have trouble with holding down the barre in exercise 37, not to worry... We've got a section later in the book to help with developing a strong barre technique. Right-hand fingerings are not included in the next few examples, so just remember to always play the low notes on the downbeats with the thumb. Using what you've already learned, choose fingers (not the thumb) that make sense for the other notes.

Exercise 35

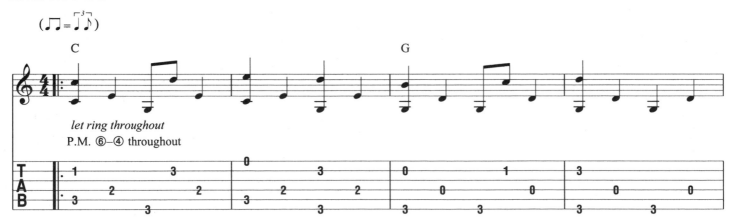

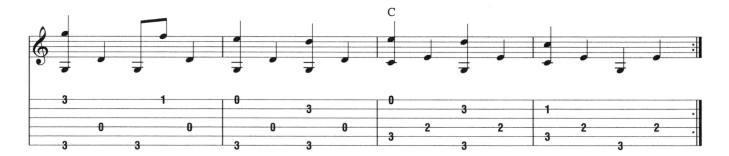

Exercise 36

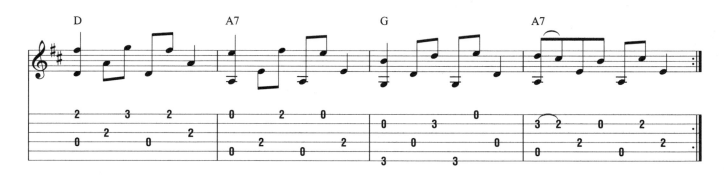

Exercise 37

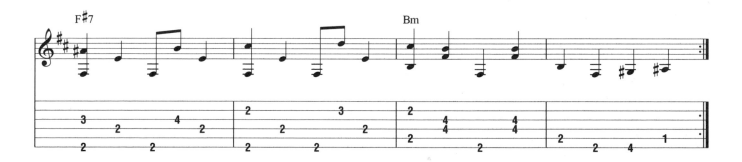

Exercise 38

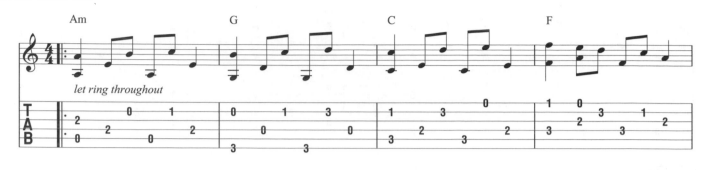

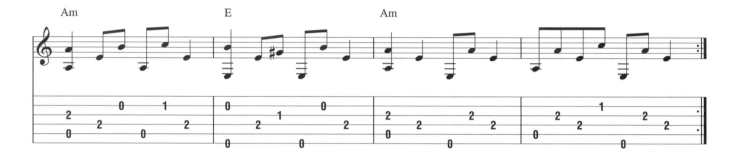

RIGHT-HAND DEXTERITY

Because fingerstyle guitar demands so much from the right hand, it is a good idea to focus some work on developing more dexterity with that hand. Of course, playing songs will help develop technique, but playing laser-focused exercises will speed the development process along. Playing arpeggios of all different varieties will definitely help your right-hand technique, but I've found that it's easy to mask some rhythmic issues and timing mistakes while playing arpeggios. The following exercise, borrowed from my classical guitar studies, will really showcase any timing and sync issues you may have with the right hand. It's based around a technique called *tremolo*, and when used with different bass notes, creates the illusion of a seamless melody.

Tremolo is a standard technique in classical guitar and refers to the very fast repetition of a single note, but the technique is rarely used in steel-string fingerstyle. The dexterity you can gain from practicing it, however, will be very beneficial. For the fingerstyle player, the purpose of working on tremolo is to develop great right-hand dexterity and rhythmic accuracy. When played in classical music, the tremolo is done at insane speeds! Of course, playing with nails on nylon strings makes this technique a bit easier. But in the world of classical guitar, it's truly a special technique that takes considerable time to master. We'll stick to a more reasonable tempo for our studies and try and reap the benefits of a more focused right-hand technique. Let's start off slowly, trying the technique on just one string.

Exercise 39

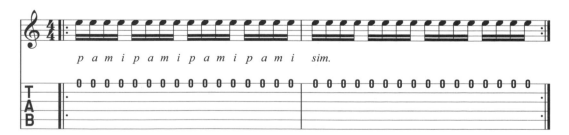

Now let's try some other strings. The first string will be the easiest for this technique, as our approach angle to the string will be clear. When we move to the inner strings, our right-hand fingers will need to be more accurate in order to miss the string above and below. The goal of these exercises isn't speed, but rather accuracy and rhythmic evenness.

Exercise 40

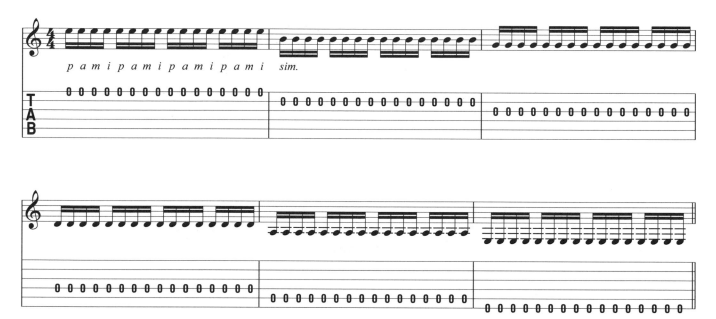

We can also use this technique with a moving bass line, creating a sort of "tremolo meets Travis picking" pattern.

Exercise 41

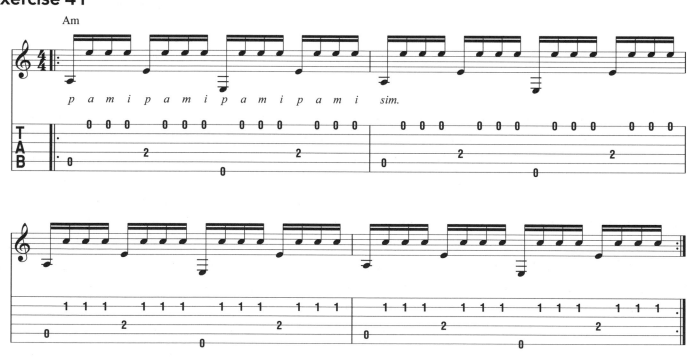

Finally, we'll give this tremolo technique the full "classical guitar" treatment and play a moving melody with changing bass notes. If you're looking for even more of a challenge, go back and play all the tremolo exercises with this new fingering: *p-i-m-a*. And for one final option, you can also try playing the tremolo studies as triplets, rather than sixteenth notes, using the following finger combinations: *p-m-a*, *p-a-m*, *p-i-m*, and *p-m-i*.

Exercise 42

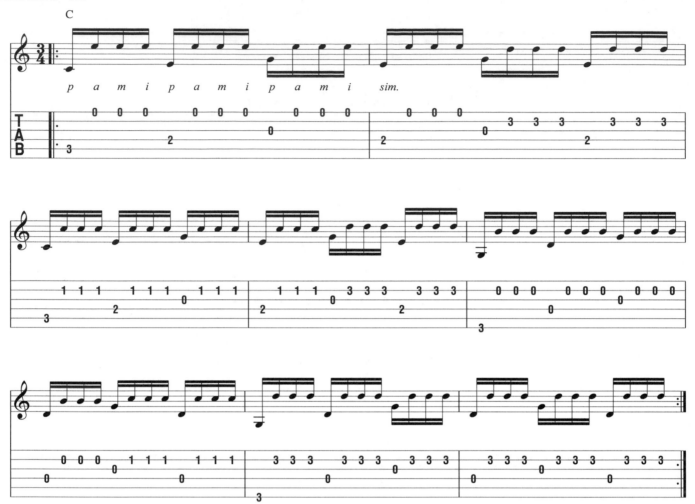

Another technique popular to classical and flamenco guitar is *rasgueado*, a strumming technique using the fingers in various patterns. Though, again, rarely used in steel-string fingerstyle guitar, the study and practice of rasgueado will be greatly beneficial to the right hand. To understand why, let's look at how the muscles work. To pluck a note, we are using flexor muscles. Because of all the practicing guitarists do, we don't need to further develop those muscles. But every time we pluck a string and use a flexor muscle, we must passively use an extensor muscle to get the finger back into position to pluck another string. If we can develop the extensor muscles more, then we should be able to get that finger back into position quickly and more efficiently. Enter the rasgueado technique—which is basically a "backwards pluck" where we strike the string with the back of the fingernail. This motion uses the extensor muscles. I find these exercises to be a great way to warm up the hand before practicing. It is also a good way to cure any muscle imbalances you may have, which often result in tendon issues. After doing these exercises for a few weeks, you should notice a more snappy-feeling right hand and an increase in speed.

In the study of classical and flamenco guitar, there are many rasgueado variations to work on. For our purposes, we are only concerned with the effect of the rasgueado on our extensor muscle development, so we'll keep the exercises rather simple. For our exercises, we'll hold down an E major chord with our right-hand thumb resting on the fifth string, but you can hold down any chord you like or even just play open strings. The music here shows notes on the top four strings, but don't worry about hitting all of them. It's really more of a percussive technique. We'll keep it slow for our purposes, but know that the real flamenco players can bust rasgueados out at crazy fast speeds with dead-on rhythm accuracy! For the right-hand fingering, *c* refers to the pinky. Let's begin with a simple quarter-note pattern (measure 1). Once you feel comfortable playing quarter notes, try adding some rhythmic flair (measure 2). We can also do a rasgueado pattern without the pinky by adding an up strum with the first finger; try to add a bit of speed to this one (measure 3).

Exercise 43

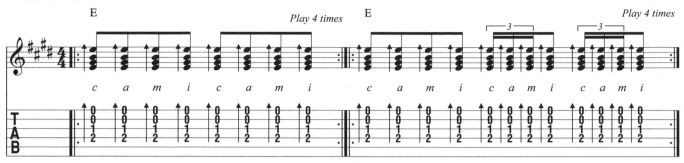

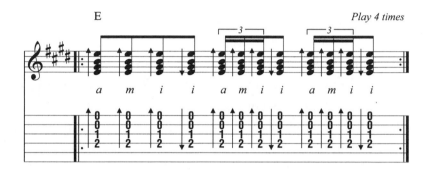

Finally, let's get the thumb in on some rasgueado action while using triplet and sextuplet patterns. We'll be using a down strum with *a* and *m* together, followed by a down strum with the thumb (*p*), and finally, completing the triplet, an up strum with the thumb (*p*). Start off very slowly and make sure your rhythm is even!

Exercise 44

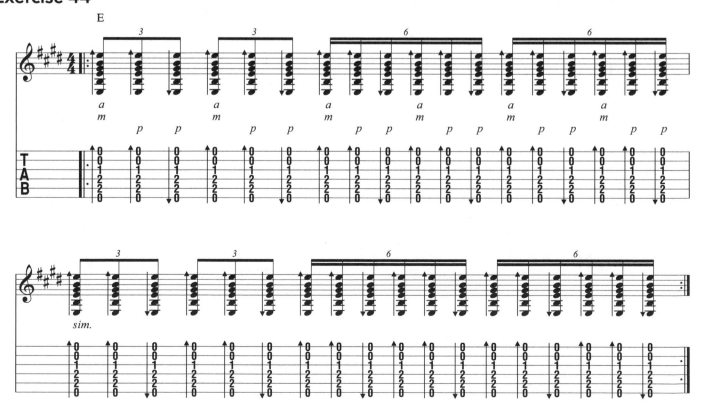

I have two final thoughts I'd like to share with you about rasgueado. Number one, these exercises don't have to be limited to the guitar. You can get the benefit of the muscle and coordination development by doing these anywhere. I find strumming on my leg to be quite effective and convenient. You can do it while watching TV, or any other time when you don't have a guitar but still have free time. Secondly, the left hand can also benefit greatly from doing rasgueados. In this case, I don't recommend doing them on guitar though, as it really isn't practical. We just need to work the muscles that open the hand, so doing them on your leg is probably the easiest. In fact, if you just make a fist and forcefully and quickly open the hand, you'll be working those same extensor muscles and you'll gain greater velocity and dexterity in the left hand as well as balancing the muscles. Just remember not to overdo it. This is like lifting weights for your hand and arm muscles, and they'll fatigue quickly.

RIGHT-HAND SPEED

Developing speed in the right hand is important for being able to play fast passages. It's not only the velocity in the right hand that will come into play, but also how well the right and left hands are synced together. You can have the fastest hands around, but if they're not synced together, things will sound like a garbled mess. So instead of laying out scales and practicing with a metronome to get fast, here are some of my favorite workouts to get my hands playing together when I feel my speed is getting sloppy. As always, work on these slowly at first, making sure all notes are played evenly and cleanly. It's the continued practice that pays dividends. There's no magic bullet. Make these exercises part of your daily routine and you'll see results in a week or two. Keep pushing the speed for further development, always minding the accuracy. The main alternating fingers we'll use are *i-m*, and you can practice starting with either finger. Also, try other combinations: *m-a*, *i-a*, or the Chet Atkins favorite *p-i* or *p-m*. (Chet would also use *p-i-m* variations to play three notes per string.) To add some variation and interest, play this pattern on all the strings or try starting it on a higher fret than shown.

Exercise 45

Here's a variation that adds a little more speed to the changing notes. Again, try the exercise on every string, in different positions on the neck, and with different right-hand fingerings.

Exercise 46

LEFT HAND

SCALES AND MELODIES OVER BASS NOTES

One of the more challenging aspects of playing fingerstyle guitar is that many times we'll be required to hold down a bass note while the melody notes above change. If you're just used to playing either single-note lines or chords, this can feel very odd, but we've already experienced it a bit when playing some of the exercises that focused on melody notes outside the chord.

In this next section, we'll strip the concept down to the bare minimum to really focus on the basic movements of holding down one note while playing a melody. Use what you've learned so far to choose good right-hand fingerings, but really try to concentrate on the left hand—make sure those bass notes ring clearly for the full value and resist that urge to pick up the finger.

Exercise 47

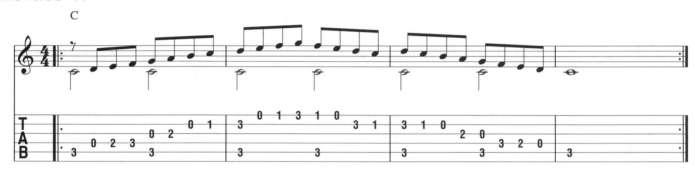

Exercise 48

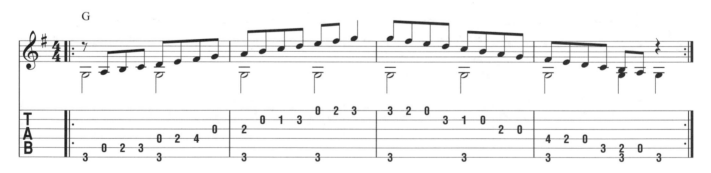

This next exercise requires you to hold down a barre while playing a scale above as the melody.

Exercise 49

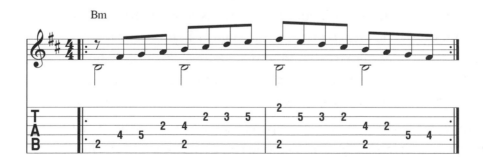

Adding some hammer-ons and pull-offs can even further challenge the left hand.

Exercise 50

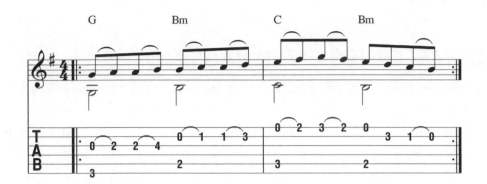

For the ultimate challenge, we'll combine hammer-ons and pulls-offs while holding down a barre. This one takes a lot of strength and dexterity, so be patient!

Exercise 51

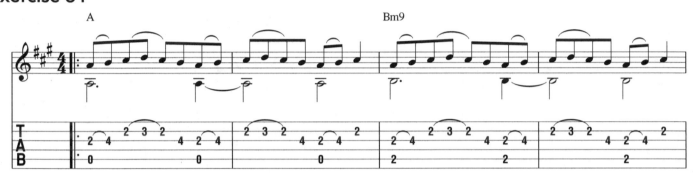

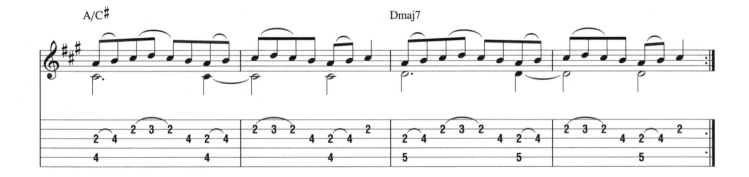

LEGATO TECHNIQUES

Notes played with *legato* sound smooth and connected. Legato techniques for guitar mainly involve the use of hammer-ons and pull-offs. Using these techniques on an acoustic steel-string guitar requires a bit more strength than on an electric guitar due to the heavier strings and slightly higher action of a steel-string guitar. While general repertoire practice will help develop the hand to play these techniques, I find it beneficial to include a more focused approach. Following are some exercises that I've used throughout the years to help develop extra strength and dexterity for legato techniques. As always, start off slowly and strive for no tension in the hand.

This first legato study makes for a great warmup exercise as well. For variety and more endurance work, play it through and then repeat, moving the position up one fret each time. (On the first repeat, start on fret 2; on the second repeat, start on fret 3; and so on.) For the next two exercises, continue using the same left-hand fingerings until you see a new pattern; then, switch over and continue to use that new pattern.

Exercise 52

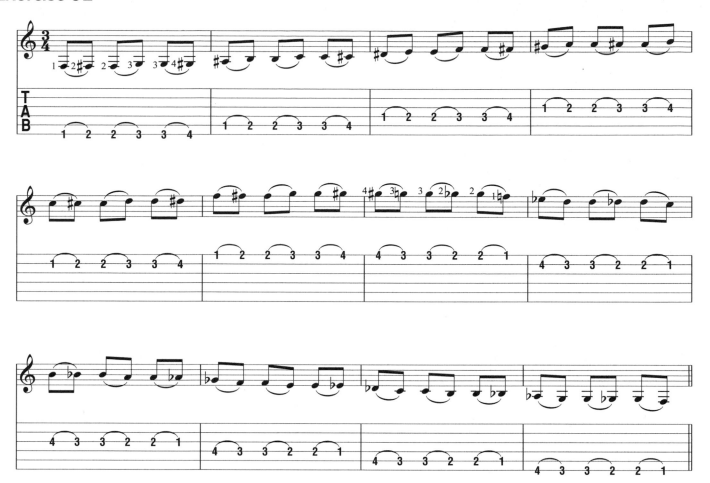

The next exercise is a great one for that weaker and often-neglected pinky finger. Again, try repeating the exercise, moving up one fret on each repeat.

Exercise 53

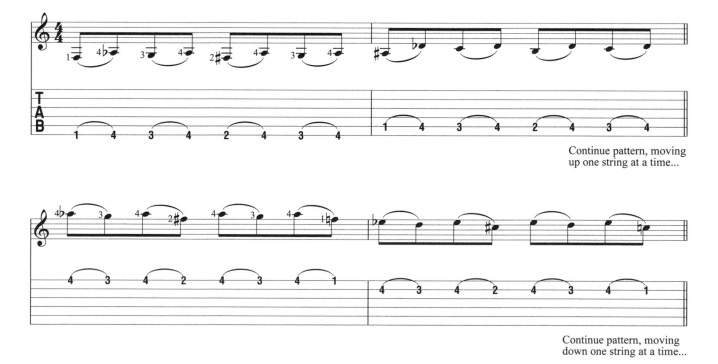

Continue pattern, moving
up one string at a time...

Continue pattern, moving
down one string at a time...

Lining up a plucked bass note with the second note of a hammer-on or pull-off is one of the more challenging things to do on the guitar. Timing is critical here because the second note of the slur and the bass note need to be heard at exactly the same time. This technique comes up often enough in repertoire pieces, so it's worth putting in some time to perfect it. It will most likely feel clumsy when starting off, and the notes might not line up exactly at first. The tendency is to rush the hammer-on or pull-off, so be mindful of that. Proceed slowly and pay close attention to the timing.

Exercise 54

Exercise 55

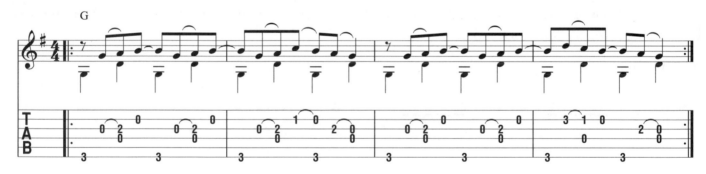

This next example uses a compound hammer-on/pull-off move. It's a little trickier to nail the timing, so try to remain focused on playing the notes in sync.

Exercise 56

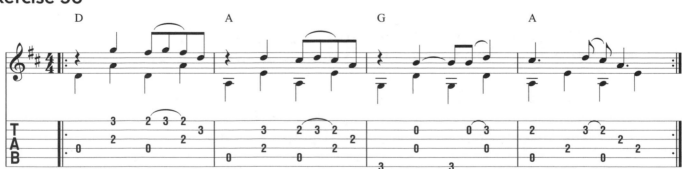

Finally, let's add a barre technique to the mix.

Exercise 57

FINGER INDEPENDENCE

One of the biggest challenges with playing fingerstyle guitar is that we often need to change chords or intervals quickly and frequently. And unlike strumming, where we can keep the beat going and use muting or open-string strumming to ease the transition, changing chords in fingerstyle almost always needs to be smooth and seamless. What follows is my favorite exercise for building finger independence, which will help with changing chords quickly. I call it the "mirror image" exercise because it involves playing an interval and then essentially playing the "opposite" or "reverse" interval (as it appears on the fretboard, not in a musical sense). It's a progressive exercise as you keep skipping more strings, making the stretch more difficult. At first, you might not be able to stretch all the way from the first string to the fifth or sixth string. Just keep working on what you can do and keep pushing ahead. The goal is to be able to form the interval "in the air" first and then place the fingers down together. But, when starting out, you may have to place one finger down first and then add the next, instead of placing both fingers down at the same time.

The following exercise starts on fret 5. If you're having difficulty with some of the stretches, you may want to move to a higher position where the frets are closer together. Conversely, if you'd like more of a challenge, move it down a few frets (with first position being the toughest). I think you'll find the first and second fingers of the left hand feel a lot easier to use than the third and fourth. That being said, it's always a good idea to focus on what is most difficult. Spending some extra time on the hard stuff is a great recipe for improvement.

Exercise 58

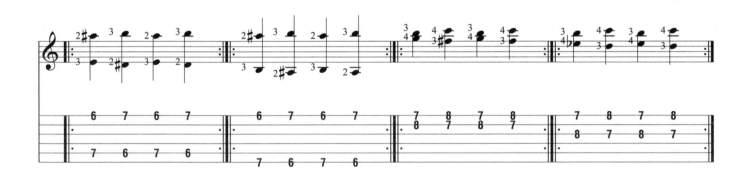

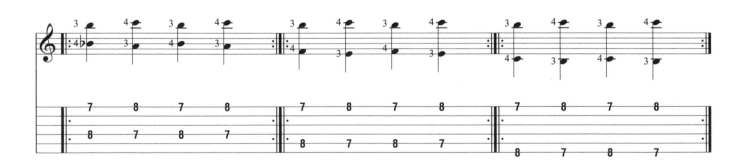

LEFT-HAND STRETCHES

There will be times when a piece of music requires us to stretch the left-hand fingers past our comfort zone. It may seem impossible at first to not only perform this stretch comfortably but even to do it at all! Luckily, stretch development happens much faster than speed development. Getting faster on the guitar can take months and years, but getting the fingers to comfortably stretch more can happen in less than a week. While the common excuse might be "I have small hands," I've found that not to be valid. I've worked with ten-year-old students who can easily perform stretches that some adults find difficult simply because the younger students worked on developing the stretch.

Here's a progressive exercise using chords. Keep all fingers down and only move one finger at a time when necessary. Make sure all notes are ringing clearly.

Exercise 59

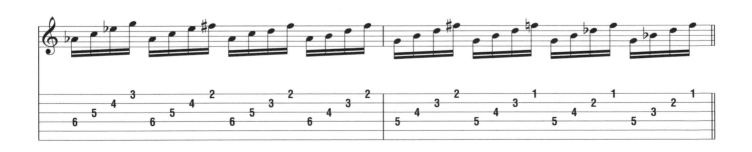

Following is a nice progressive exercise that develops the stretch by working on one string. The pattern starts high up the neck and works down one fret upon each repetition of the fourteen-note pattern,, becoming more difficult as the frets get further apart. Hold each lower finger down as you play the higher note in the two-note groups; for example, hold the first finger down through the first three beats. For even more of a challenge, leave the fingers on the fretboard below each new two-note group as you progress through each measure.

Exercise 60

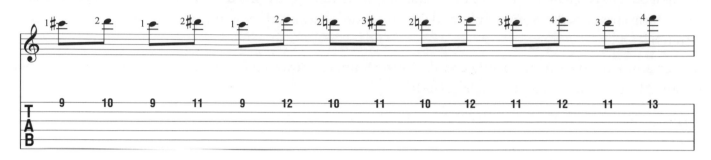

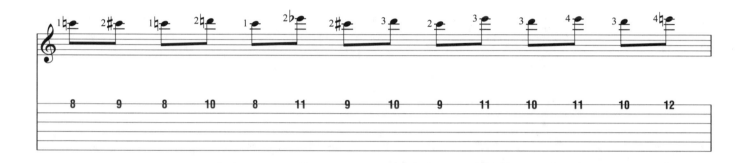

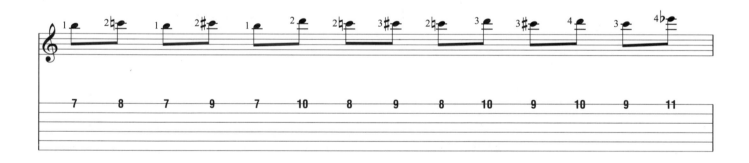

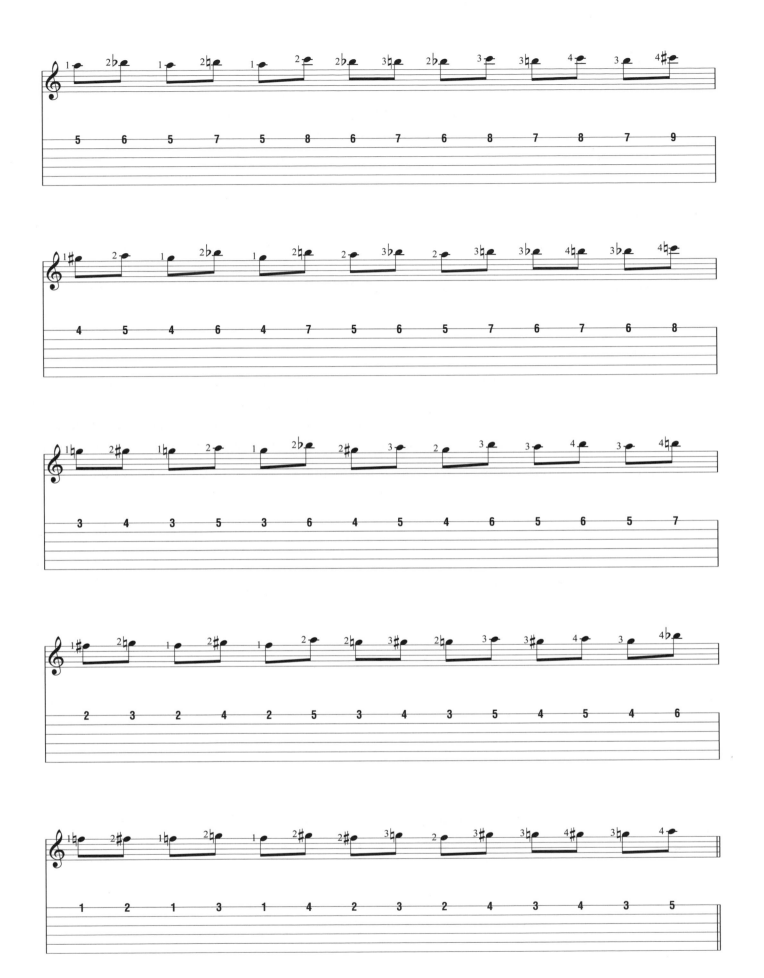

BARRE TECHNIQUE

The *barre* technique, fretting multiple strings with one flattened finger, is one of the major hurdles to get over when learning the guitar. Many students will avoid it at first, as it can be very frustrating. While it does require a bit of strength, more importantly, it requires very accurate finger placement. We've assumed that you can already use the barre technique to some extent, as some of the exercises we've already seen have used it. So, we won't start from the beginning but rather will look at some tips and exercises to help make your barre technique stronger and more comfortable to use.

Before we try an exercise, there are a few tips that I've found can really help with the barre. The first tip is: instead of fretting down the middle of the inside of the finger, think of rolling the finger a bit towards the headstock of the guitar. You'll notice that the fingers naturally bend toward the palm with ease but don't bend in the same direction as easily when rolled to the side—that's the way our knuckle joints work. If you can contact the fretboard more with the side of your barring finger, you'll have a little extra help in keeping that finger absolutely straight. Also, make sure that your finger joints don't line up with a string, as the small creases at the joints provide limited pressure and might cause a string to buzz.

The second tip has more to do with where your grip strength comes from. If you try to exert extra pressure between your thumb and fingers, you'll find the muscles tire and cramp rather quickly. But if you can think of using the larger muscles of your shoulder, you'll have strength to spare. To do this, imagine pulling the guitar back with your left arm while keeping it braced against your body with your right arm resting on the top edge of the guitar.

Now, we'll try some exercises to help get you comfortable with the barre. Most times, simply holding a barre is not a problem, but holding a strong barre while the other fingers fret on and off to play a melody can be tricky.

Exercise 61

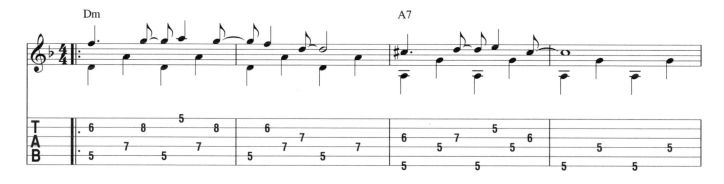

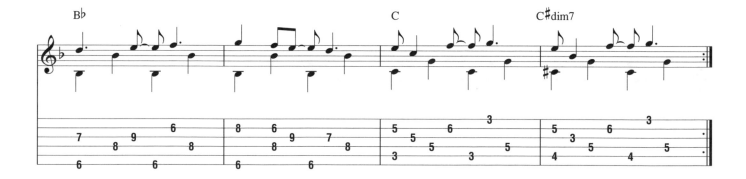

This next exercise includes the challenge of using legato techniques over the barre.

Exercise 62

We can really turn it up a notch by holding down a note with the third finger. The following exercise makes for a great pinky workout since the third finger is held down on fret 7 of the fourth string and the pinky handles the melody notes. Feel free to move the exercise around the neck to work on your barre in other positions.

Exercise 63

In most cases, we'll use the first finger to barre, but occasionally we might need to barre with the other fingers—especially fingers 3 and 4. You might have noticed that barring with the third finger is a popular way to play the major-chord shape rooted on the fifth string—the "moveable A shape." Luckily, we'll only be barring a few strings, as opposed to all six, but the same rules apply. Keep the finger straight and use the weight of the arm and shoulder to gain extra leverage. Try this exercise which incorporates some third- and fourth-finger barres as well as a great stretch.

Exercise 64

FRETTING NOTES WITH THE THUMB

In order to play certain chords or to free up fingers for a melody, sometimes we'll call on the left-hand thumb to do some fretting over the neck. This can be an awkward experience if you've never tried it. It also contradicts what we work on when first learning the guitar, which is to keep the thumb behind the neck. That being said, it can become a great trick to have in your bag. Those of you with smaller hands or shorter thumbs may be at a bit of a disadvantage, but give it some time. It's well worth the effort.

One of the most common chords to fret with the thumb is the D/F♯ chord in open position. Try fretting the low F♯ with the thumb in the next example.

Exercise 65

Another common chord to grab with the thumb over the top is the barred G-chord shape with its root on the low E string. Any major barre chord with its root on the sixth string can be played using the thumb. Playing with the thumb allows us to have an extra finger available for melody notes since, in the case of this chord, we don't have to use a finger to barre. By using this shape and lifting the second finger, we can play an Fsus2 chord with a low F bass note on fret 1 of the sixth string. Without using the thumb, this chord would be very awkward to finger, and we would not have an extra finger available for melody notes.

Exercise 66

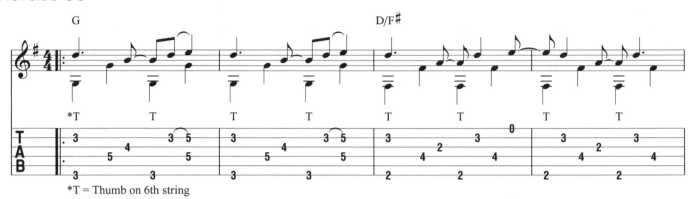

*T = Thumb on 6th string

There are no rules as far as what chords you should fret with the thumb. If you're comfortable with the technique, feel free to use it often. It's not just used by fingerstyle players either. Check out any video of Jimi Hendrix, Stevie Ray Vaughan, or John Mayer. They're almost always playing barre chord shapes with the thumb and even using it to fret some notes while soloing. In fact, in rock and blues playing, the thumb is not only used to fret notes but also to mute the sixth (and sometimes the fifth) string. That thumb-muting technique can also be helpful when you're strumming a chord and don't want the sixth or fifth string to ring. I won't lie, having large hands definitely helps. And if you're really struggling with the technique, you can always find a way to play a passage differently without using the thumb. Just remember, new techniques take time to develop, so don't give up if you can't get it right away.

BUILD A FINGERSTYLE ARRANGEMENT

Now that we've discussed and worked on our technical abilities, let's put our skills to use and make some music! In general, a fingerstyle piece will include a melody above some sort of chord and bass-note accompaniment. You can create an original melody and put chords around it, or you can come up with a chord pattern and create a melody that fits. It's safe to say that a knowledge of music theory is helpful when working on arrangements (although not necessary). It's beyond the scope of this book to delve too deep into music theory, so I'll try to present the material in a simple and easy-to-understand format. We'll take a look at a few popular melodies and explore some ideas on how to put together a great solo fingerstyle arrangement. Let's start with a melody you're probably familiar with: Beethoven's "Ode to Joy."

"Ode to Joy"
Melody Only

After playing through the melody, the first thing you'll want to do is look at the chords provided above the music. In general, it's best to let the melody note be the highest note in the chord. This will help the melody to stand out. So, the simplest idea for fingerstyle arrangement is to play a chord voicing that includes the melody note as the highest note in the chord. This is where your music theory and chord knowledge will be helpful. Fortunately, in "Ode to Joy," the chords are simple and can all be played in open position. Later in this section, we'll look at how to deal with more complicated voicings, but for now, let's add some chords to this melody. Hold down as much of the chord as possible and let the notes ring throughout.

"Ode to Joy"
Melody/Chord

Did you notice the few times where the melody note wasn't part of the chord? In those cases, we still started with a basic chord shape and just added the melody note on top. Take a look at the G chord in the fourth measure and the F chord in the sixth measure. With the added notes, these chords essentially became G6 and Fadd9 chords, respectively. This happens often in arranging. You need to have a good visual concept of the chords and where melody notes can be added. There are no rules to doing this. You simply want to come up with chord voicings that include the melody notes on the top. In the next exercise, try to hold the basic chord shape down, letting the notes of the chord ring while you play the melody notes.

Now let's take our arrangement one step further and add some flavor… "Travis style." We'll use Travis picking and pull a simple bass line from the chords. The F chords may be played with a barre, like in the video, or you can try using the thumb over the top technique that we saw earlier. There will be other spots in the upcoming arrangements where fretting with the thumb might be worth a try.

"Ode to Joy"
Travis Picking

For the final treatment of "Ode to Joy," we'll add some accompaniment notes to the melody section. Notice that this creates a predictable and repeatable pattern for the right hand. Although the music sounds complex, it's not that difficult to play. Again, there are no rules on how to create an arrangement. Use your ear and your knowledge of theory, and get creative by experimenting with new ideas.

"Ode to Joy"
Fingerstyle Arrangement

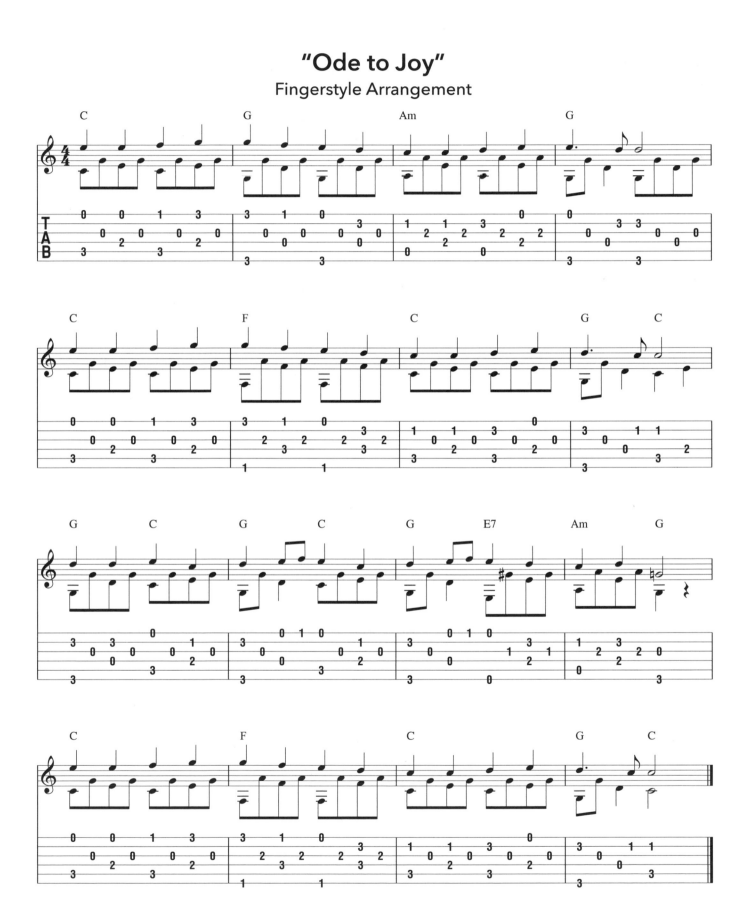

Let's look at another arrangement using the popular Christmas song "Jingle Bells." First, start with the melody.

"Jingle Bells"
Melody Only

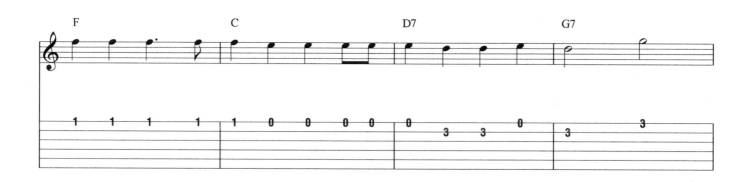

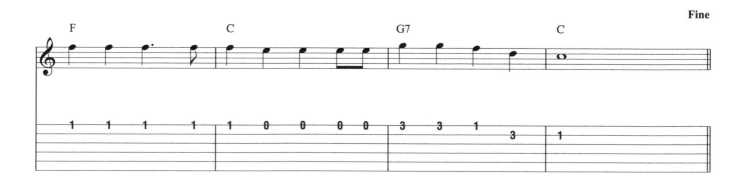

Verse

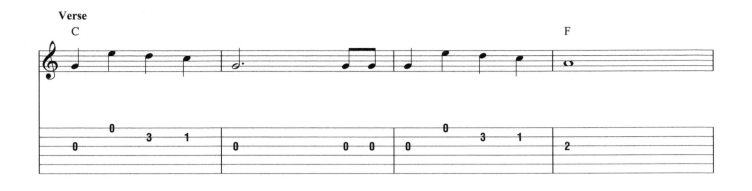

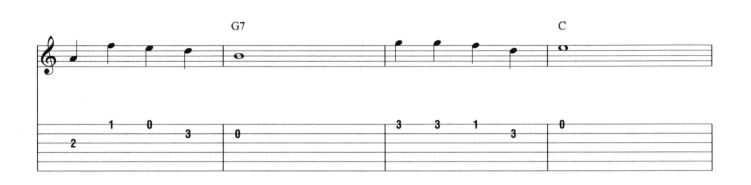

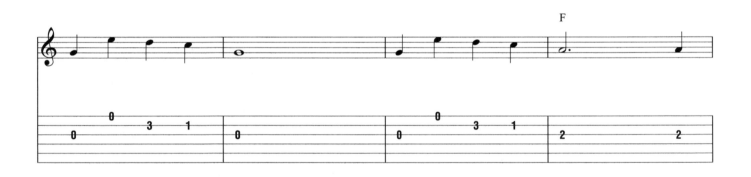

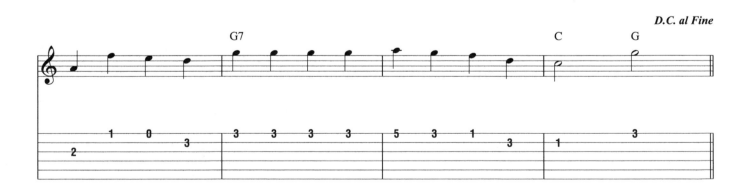

Next, let's figure out some chord voicings. Most of the chords we'll need for this arrangement can be simple open-position chords, but there are a few instances where a chord voicing in a higher position is a better option. In this arrangement, the D7 chord is played in a higher position. Again, the melody notes won't always naturally be part of the chord, but we can always start with a chord shape that we know and add the melody note on top. Doing this can create a nice extended harmony.

"Jingle Bells"
Melody/Chord

The chord voicings we've used so far have mostly consisted of a melody note on top with two accompaniment notes plus a bass note below, creating a full-sounding four-note chord. In some cases, it wasn't possible to use a four-note chord because a melody note ended up on a lower string. In those cases, we can settle for a three-note chord. Again, there are no rules, so let your ear be your guide. Sometimes, a bass note under a melody note is all that's needed; other times, a full chord sounds best.

In this arrangement, I chose a D7 chord in the third position with its root on the A string because I liked that I was able to include the C note in the accompaniment, bringing out the ♭7 of the D7 chord in the harmony. That same idea carried through when figuring out a position for the G7 chord. When you're figuring out chord voicings, it's a good idea to plan ahead. If you're thinking of adding a Travis-style accompaniment, make sure your chord voicing will allow you to include those extra alternating bass notes.

In the case of the F chord in measures 5 and 13 of the verse, notice that we need to perform a hinged-barre move. To do this, we pluck the high F note on the first string with the barre down, and then, while keeping our first finger on the sixth string for the low F bass note, we lift up the top portion of the barre to reveal the open E on the first string. Also note where we fretted some melody notes (for example, the F note on fret 6 of the second string in the G7 chords), allowing us to still hold down most of the chord below. Whenever possible, allowing chords to ring will help make your arrangements sound rich and full.

Finally, let's add some Travis-style accompaniment to complete our arrangement. For extra flavor, we'll throw in a short bass run between the chorus and verse. Notice how we play with the phrasing and rhythms of the melody notes, altering them a bit to better suit our pattern.

"Jingle Bells"
Travis Picking

Now let's try to put together one more song, the ever-popular "House of the Rising Sun." This is standard repertoire for many beginning guitarists who seek to learn the original arpeggiated part. For our version, we'll take this great melody and add some Travis-picking magic. First, here's the original melody played in 6/8 time.

"House of the Rising Sun"
Melody Only

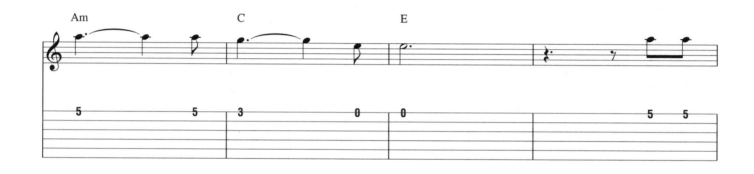

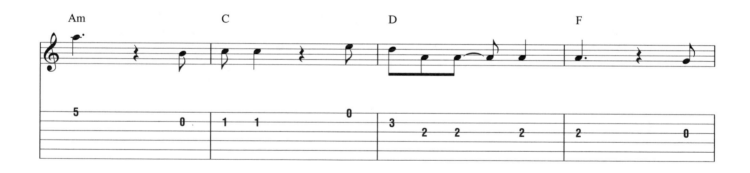

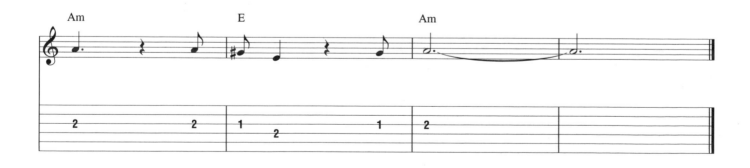

Before we add some Travis picking, let's explore the option of recreating the flavor of the original guitar part along with the melody, while keeping the 6/8 feel.

"House of the Rising Sun"
Melody/Accompaniment

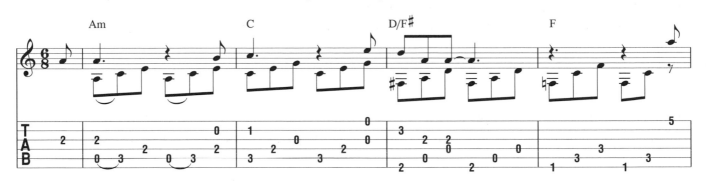

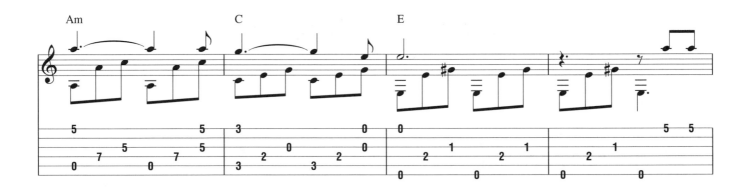

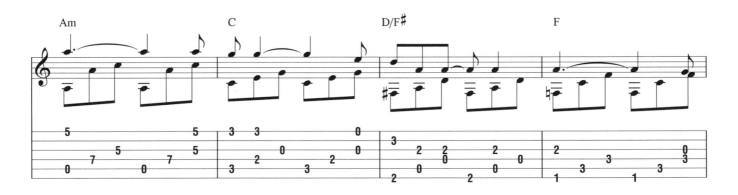

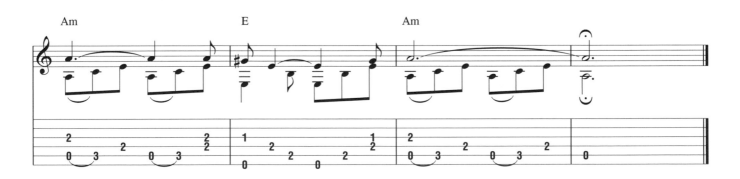

In order to keep the melody separate from the accompaniment, we need to use some different chord voicings. Notice how we voiced the Am chord in the first measure, and then, as the melody got higher, we moved it up to the fifth position. As you can see, having a good command of the fretboard and knowing chords all over the neck will be helpful in fingerstyle arranging. Also, instead of playing an awkward, stretched-out D chord, we went with a D/F#, which allowed for an easier fingering and provided a nice chromatic bass line to the F chord while still keeping the quality of the D major chord. We also altered the melody a bit in measures 9 and 10 in an attempt to make it work better with the accompaniment part. Whenever arranging for fingerstyle guitar, I find it best to always consider the playability of the piece first and foremost as opposed to nailing every detail of the melody or accompaniment. Instead of trying to recreate the original exactly, think about how you can take what's there and make it your own. Get creative!

Now let's add some Travis-picking and give this tune a new flair. We'll have to make some big alterations since the original feel is in 6/8 time, and we'll want to put it in 4/4 for a Travis-picking feel. This arrangement is a great example of the liberties you can take with rhythms and melodies.

"House of the Rising Sun"
Travis Picking

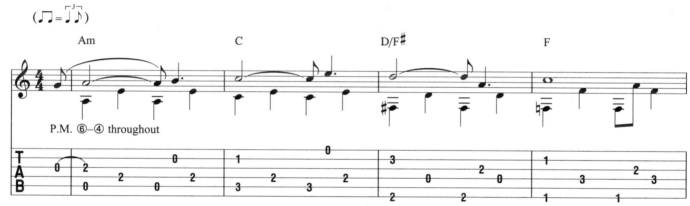

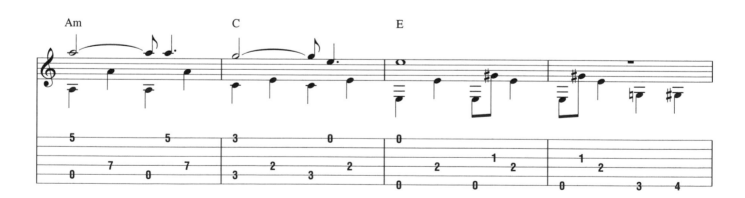

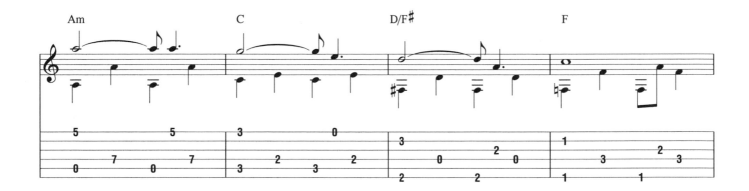

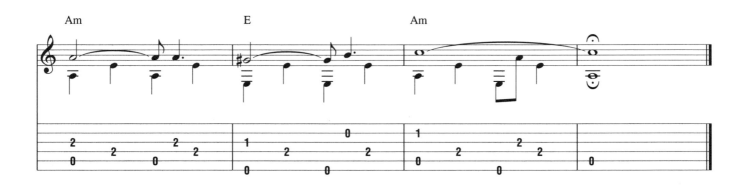

The options for creating fingerstyle arrangements are endless. You can take anything—a classical piece, a jazz tune, a pop classic, or even a heavy metal song—and use it to create a cool arrangement. Start off by learning the melody, and then take a look at the chords. At this point, you'll need to decide if the original song is in a "friendly" enough key for guitar or if you should transpose. Transposition is simply taking a melody and chord sequence and changing the pitch of the notes while keeping the relative intervals between the notes the same. For example, let's say you have a song that's in the key of B♭. That won't give you a lot of options for using open strings since most of the chords used in the key of B♭ have roots on fretted notes. Being able to use open strings along with open position chords will generally make the job easier and provide a fuller sounding arrangement. So, your first option might be to transpose the melody down to the key of A. Since moving from B♭ to A is one half step (one fret), all you'd need to do is move every melody note and chord down one fret. Another option would be to move up to the key of C. In that case, you'd be moving up a whole step (two frets), so every melody note and chord would need to be moved up two frets. Sometimes, you might find that a song needs to be transposed up or down by more than just a few frets. You'll need to experiment and try many options to see what yields the most sensible arrangement. Remember, these songs were most likely written with the vocalist's range in mind; however, when creating a solo fingerstyle arrangement, we need to instead consider what lays out best on our instrument, the guitar. When all else fails, try an alternate tuning or a capo!

TRAVIS BLUES VARIATIONS

Consider this last section to be the Travis-picking equivalent of the famous *Twenty Studies for the Guitar* by Fernando Sor, a classical guitar essential. The exercises that follow are basic blues arrangements with a simple melody and a Travis-picking accompaniment. You'll notice many of the techniques that we discussed earlier in the book show up in these pieces. Although the notation shows one repeat, these can be played over and over "until your hand falls off." Since they are based on the blues, they can really be played at any tempo and still sound authentic. Start off slowly and build your speed to a blistering level, always making sure your rhythm is accurate and steady and the melody is clear and precise. They make for a great warm up or, if played repeatedly, an excellent workout in endurance.

"Travis Blues #1" makes use of some two- and three-finger chords to bring out the melody. It is a great study in right-hand finger independence as well as left-hand reach. I opted to voice the A chord with an open fifth string bass note, but if you want more of a challenge or the ability to move the song to a different key, you can play the A chord as a barre chord with the bass note on the sixth string. Imagine the melody played by a horn section to feel the song dynamically.

"Travis Blues #1"

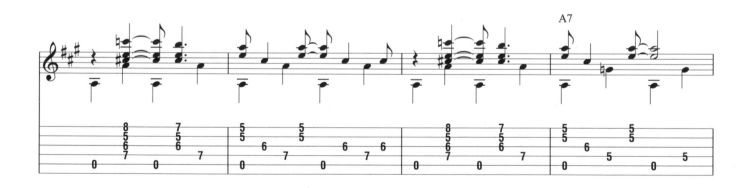

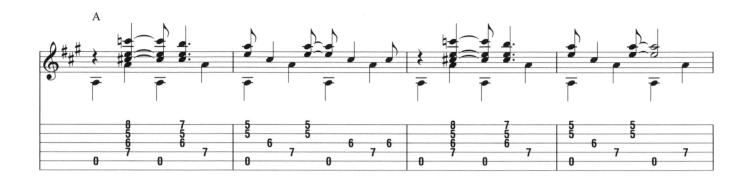

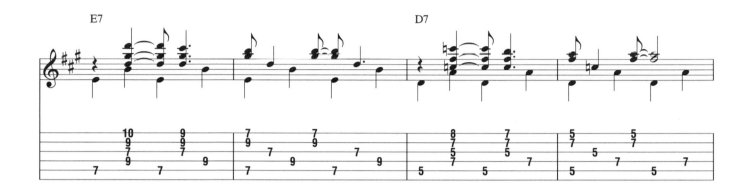

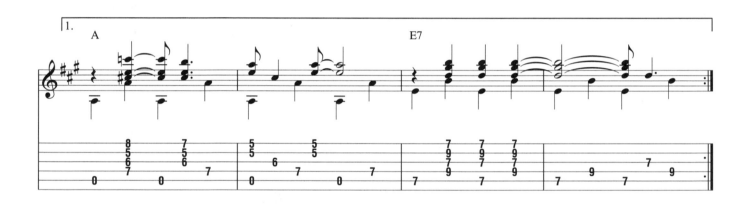

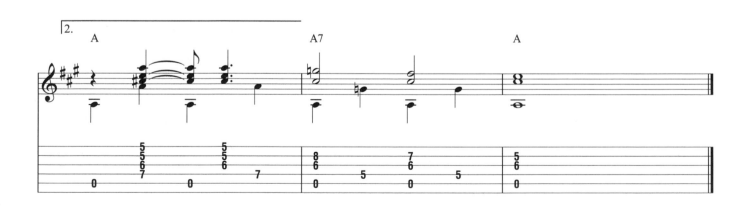

"Travis Blues #2" makes use of three-string Travis-style picking patterns in the bass line. This can get confusing and difficult when played with a melody on top. Take some time to practice just the thumb part to help ingrain the correct pattern. Also, note the quarter-step bends on some melody notes. Those are slight bends, just enough to push the note out of tune a bit but not enough to get a full half-step rise in pitch. Make sure your other fingers stay solidly in place as you bend the selected string.

"Travis Blues #2"

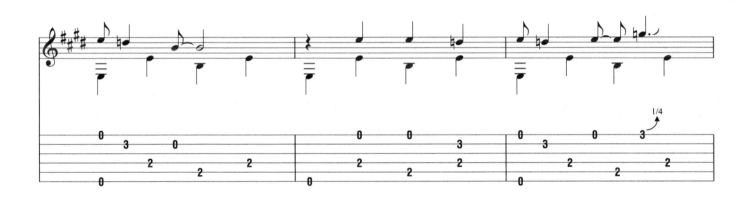

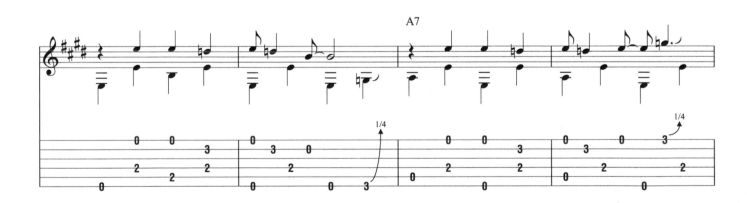

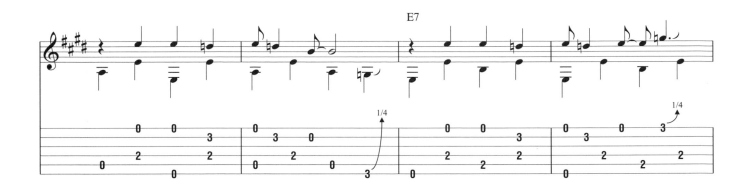

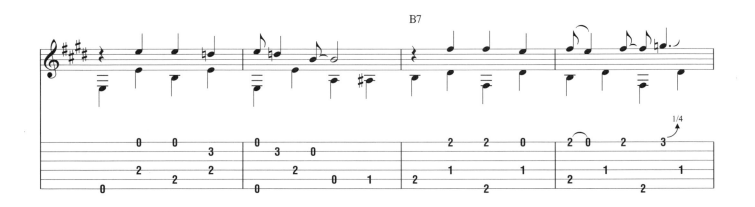

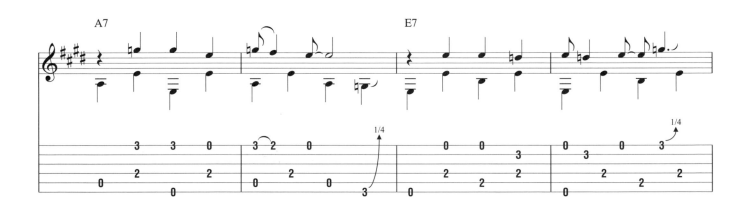

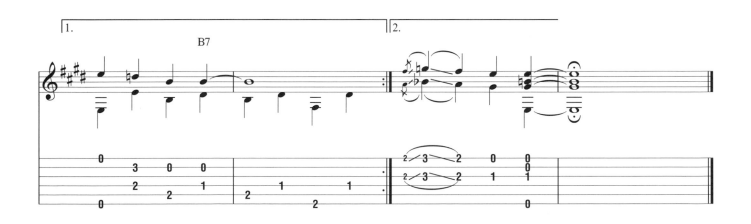

"Travis Blues #3" is a fun piece for working on your speed. Once you get the pattern down, you can really crank up the tempo. Make sure the hammer-ons and pull-offs are clean, and the thumb is keeping a solid rhythm.

"Travis Blues #3"

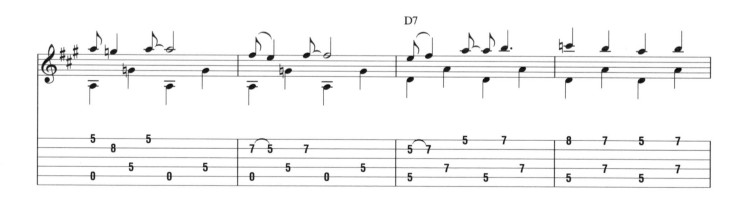

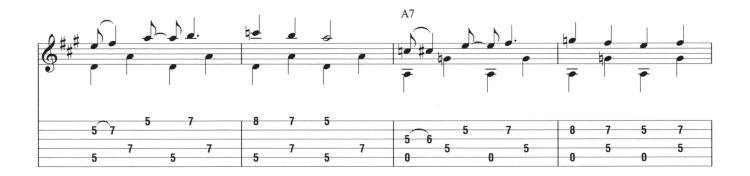

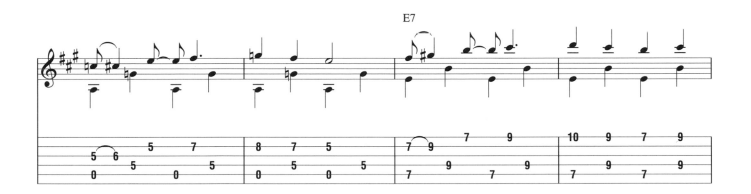

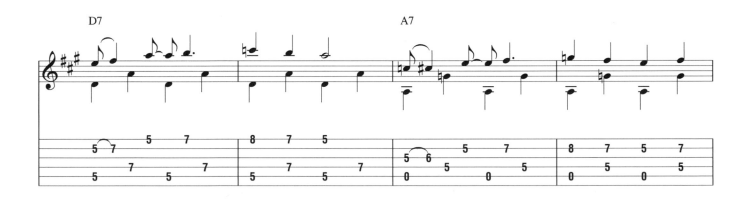

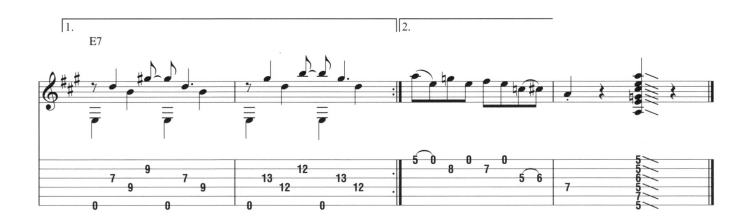

"Travis Blues #4" makes use of hammer-ons over bass notes. It's played entirely with barre chords, so feel free to move it around the neck to play in different keys. If you're having difficulty with the barre, remember to keep that first finger straight, roll it a bit to the side, and move it up or down to find that sweet spot where the finger joint creases don't line up with a string. If your hand is cramping by the end of the tune, be patient. It takes time to build up the strength and endurance to play a full song with barre chords.

"Travis Blues #4"

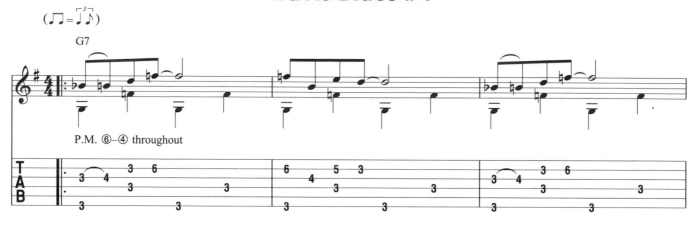

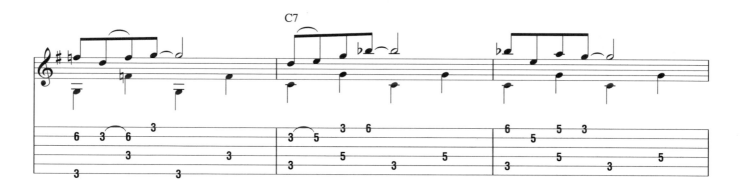

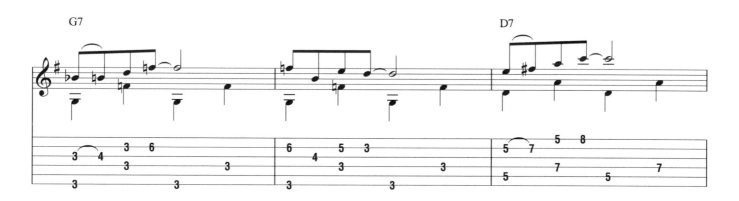

IN CONCLUSION

I sincerely hope you have enjoyed this book and have found it helpful in your journey with fingerstyle guitar. Take these exercises and concepts and use them while digging into the vast repertoire of fingerstyle guitar that exists. Find those tunes that bring you joy and play them over and over. Never doubt your ability to master even the most difficult of pieces. They're just notes, and time conquers all. Be patient and keep a positive "you can do it" attitude. We hear these amazing pieces and only see the finished product, not the hours, weeks, months, and years it took the performer to get that piece to that level. Remember, at some point everybody struggled to play a C chord.

It was a pleasure for me to look back at my journey and share with you the things that I felt helped me achieve my goals. But remember, learning the guitar is a journey and you must enjoy the process. We will never master it, but forever chase that dream.

—Doug Boduch

GUITAR NOTATION LEGEND

Guitar music can be notated three different ways: on a *musical staff*, in *tablature*, and in *rhythm slashes*.

RHYTHM SLASHES are written above the staff. Strum chords in the rhythm indicated. Use the chord diagrams found at the top of the first page of the transcription for the appropriate chord voicings. Round noteheads indicate single notes.

THE MUSICAL STAFF shows pitches and rhythms and is divided by bar lines into measures. Pitches are named after the first seven letters of the alphabet.

TABLATURE graphically represents the guitar fingerboard. Each horizontal line represents a string, and each number represents a fret.

4th string, 2nd fret   1st & 2nd strings open, played together   open D chord

Definitions for Special Guitar Notation

HALF-STEP BEND: Strike the note and bend up 1/2 step.

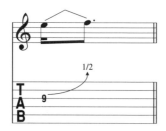

WHOLE-STEP BEND: Strike the note and bend up one step.

GRACE NOTE BEND: Strike the note and immediately bend up as indicated.

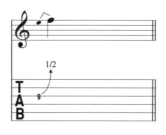

SLIGHT (MICROTONE) BEND: Strike the note and bend up 1/4 step.

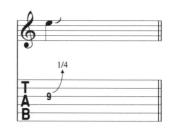

BEND AND RELEASE: Strike the note and bend up as indicated, then release back to the original note. Only the first note is struck.

PRE-BEND: Bend the note as indicated, then strike it.

PRE-BEND AND RELEASE: Bend the note as indicated. Strike it and release the bend back to the original note.

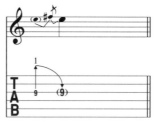

UNISON BEND: Strike the two notes simultaneously and bend the lower note up to the pitch of the higher.

VIBRATO: The string is vibrated by rapidly bending and releasing the note with the fretting hand.

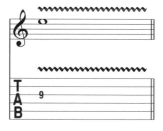

WIDE VIBRATO: The pitch is varied to a greater degree by vibrating with the fretting hand.

HAMMER-ON: Strike the first (lower) note with one finger, then sound the higher note (on the same string) with another finger by fretting it without picking.

PULL-OFF: Place both fingers on the notes to be sounded. Strike the first note and without picking, pull the finger off to sound the second (lower) note.

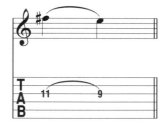

LEGATO SLIDE: Strike the first note and then slide the same fret-hand finger up or down to the second note. The second note is not struck.

SHIFT SLIDE: Same as legato slide, except the second note is struck.

TRILL: Very rapidly alternate between the notes indicated by continuously hammering on and pulling off.

TAPPING: Hammer ("tap") the fret indicated with the pick-hand index or middle finger and pull off to the note fretted by the fret hand.

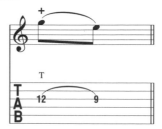

NATURAL HARMONIC: Strike the note while the fret-hand lightly touches the string directly over the fret indicated.

Harm.

PINCH HARMONIC: The note is fretted normally and a harmonic is produced by adding the edge of the thumb or the tip of the index finger of the pick hand to the normal pick attack.

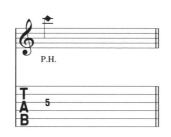

P.H.

HARP HARMONIC: The note is fretted normally and a harmonic is produced by gently resting the pick hand's index finger directly above the indicated fret (in parentheses) while the pick hand's thumb or pick assists by plucking the appropriate string.

H.H.

PICK SCRAPE: The edge of the pick is rubbed down (or up) the string, producing a scratchy sound.

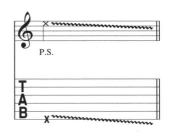

P.S.

MUFFLED STRINGS: A percussive sound is produced by laying the fret hand across the string(s) without depressing, and striking them with the pick hand.

PALM MUTING: The note is partially muted by the pick hand lightly touching the string(s) just before the bridge.

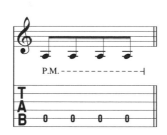

P.M.

RAKE: Drag the pick across the strings indicated with a single motion.

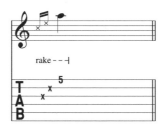

rake

TREMOLO PICKING: The note is picked as rapidly and continuously as possible.

ARPEGGIATE: Play the notes of the chord indicated by quickly rolling them from bottom to top.

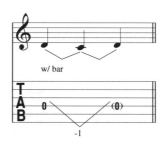

VIBRATO BAR DIVE AND RETURN: The pitch of the note or chord is dropped a specified number of steps (in rhythm), then returned to the original pitch.

w/ bar

VIBRATO BAR SCOOP: Depress the bar just before striking the note, then quickly release the bar.

w/ bar

VIBRATO BAR DIP: Strike the note and then immediately drop a specified number of steps, then release back to the original pitch.

w/ bar

Additional Musical Definitions

(accent)
- Accentuate note (play it louder).

(accent)
- Accentuate note with great intensity.

(staccato)
- Play the note short.

⊓
- Downstroke

∨
- Upstroke

D.S. al Coda
- Go back to the sign (𝄋), then play until the measure marked "*To Coda*," then skip to the section labelled "**Coda**."

D.C. al Fine
- Go back to the beginning of the song and play until the measure marked "*Fine*" (end).

Rhy. Fig.
- Label used to recall a recurring accompaniment pattern (usually chordal).

Riff
- Label used to recall composed, melodic lines (usually single notes) which recur.

Fill
- Label used to identify a brief melodic figure which is to be inserted into the arrangement.

Rhy. Fill
- A chordal version of a Fill.

tacet
- Instrument is silent (drops out).

- Repeat measures between signs.

- When a repeated section has different endings, play the first ending only the first time and the second ending only the second time.

NOTE: Tablature numbers in parentheses mean:
1. The note is being sustained over a system (note in standard notation is tied), or
2. The note is sustained, but a new articulation (such as a hammer-on, pull-off, slide or vibrato) begins, or
3. The note is a barely audible "ghost" note (note in standard notation is also in parentheses).

Get Better at Guitar

...with these Great Guitar Instruction Books from Hal Leonard!

101 GUITAR TIPS
STUFF ALL THE PROS KNOW AND USE
by Adam St. James
This book contains invaluable guidance on everything from scales and music theory to truss rod adjustments, proper recording studio set-ups, and much more.
00695737 Book/Online Audio $17.99

AMAZING PHRASING
by Tom Kolb
This book/audio pack explores all the main components necessary for crafting well-balanced rhythmic and melodic phrases. It also explains how these phrases are put together to form cohesive solos. The companion audio contains 89 demo tracks, most with full-band backing.
00695583 Book/Online Audio $22.99

ARPEGGIOS FOR THE MODERN GUITARIST
by Tom Kolb
Using this no-nonsense book with online audio, guitarists will learn to apply and execute all types of arpeggio forms using a variety of techniques, including alternate picking, sweep picking, tapping, string skipping, and legato.
00695862 Book/Online Audio $22.99

BLUES YOU CAN USE
by John Ganapes
This comprehensive source for learning blues guitar is designed to develop both your lead and rhythm playing. Includes: 21 complete solos • blues chords, progressions and riffs • turnarounds • movable scales and soloing techniques • string bending • utilizing the entire fingerboard • and more.
00142420 Book/Online Media..................$22.99

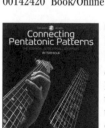

CONNECTING PENTATONIC PATTERNS
by Tom Kolb
If you've been finding yourself trapped in the pentatonic box, this book is for you! This hands-on book with online audio offers examples for guitar players of all levels, from beginner to advanced. Study this book faithfully, and soon you'll be soloing all over the neck with the greatest of ease.
00696445 Book/Online Audio $24.99

FRETBOARD MASTERY
by Troy Stetina
Untangle the mysterious regions of the guitar fretboard and unlock your potential. This book familiarizes you with all the shapes you need to know by applying them in real musical examples, thereby reinforcing and reaffirming your newfound knowledge.
00695331 Book/Online Audio $22.99

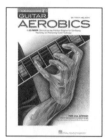

GUITAR AEROBICS
by Troy Nelson
Here is a daily dose of guitar "vitamins" to keep your chops fine tuned! Musical styles include rock, blues, jazz, metal, country, and funk. Techniques taught include alternate picking, arpeggios, sweep picking, string skipping, legato, string bending, and rhythm guitar.
00695946 Book/Online Audio $24.99

GUITAR CLUES
OPERATION PENTATONIC
by Greg Koch
Whether you're new to improvising or have been doing it for a while, this book/audio pack will provide loads of delicious licks and tricks that you can use right away, from volume swells and chicken pickin' to intervallic and chordal ideas.
00695827 Book/Online Audio $24.99

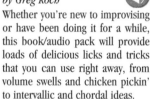

PAT METHENY – GUITAR ETUDES
Over the years, in many master classes and workshops around the world, Pat has demonstrated the kind of daily workout he puts himself through. This book includes a collection of 14 guitar etudes he created to help you limber up, improve picking technique and build finger independence.
00696587..................$19.99

PICTURE CHORD ENCYCLOPEDIA
This comprehensive guitar chord resource for all playing styles and levels features five voicings of 44 chord qualities for all twelve keys – 2,640 chords in all! For each, there is a clearly illustrated chord frame, as well as *an actual photo* of the chord being played!.
00695224..................$22.99

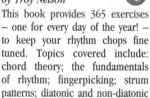

RHYTHM GUITAR 365
by Troy Nelson
This book provides 365 exercises – one for every day of the year! – to keep your rhythm chops fine tuned. Topics covered include: chord theory; the fundamentals of rhythm; fingerpicking; strum patterns; diatonic and non-diatonic progressions; triads; major and minor keys; and more.
00103627 Book/Online Audio $27.99

SCALE CHORD RELATIONSHIPS
by Michael Mueller & Jeff Schroedl
This book/audio pack explains how to: recognize keys • analyze chord progressions • use the modes • play over nondiatonic harmony • use harmonic and melodic minor scales • use symmetrical scales • incorporate exotic scales • and much more!
00695563 Book/Online Audio $17.99

SPEED MECHANICS FOR LEAD GUITAR
by Troy Stetina
Take your playing to the stratosphere with this advanced lead book which will help you develop speed and precision in today's explosive playing styles. Learn the fastest ways to achieve speed and control, secrets to make your practice time really count, and how to open your ears and make your musical ideas more solid and tangible.
00699323 Book/Online Audio $22.99

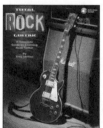

TOTAL ROCK GUITAR
by Troy Stetina
This comprehensive source for learning rock guitar is designed to develop both lead and rhythm playing. It covers: getting a tone that rocks • open chords, power chords and barre chords • riffs, scales and licks • string bending, strumming, and harmonics • and more.
00695246 Book/Online Audio $22.99

Guitar World Presents STEVE VAI'S GUITAR WORKOUT
In this book, Steve Vai reveals his path to virtuoso enlightenment with two challenging guitar workouts – one 10-hour and one 30-hour – which include scale and chord exercises, ear training, sight-reading, music theory, and much more.
00119643..................$16.99

HAL•LEONARD®

Prices, contents, and availability subject to change without notice.

Order these and more publications from your favorite music retailer at
halleonard.com

0423
032